Original title:
Endless Days in Paradise

Copyright © 2025 Creative Arts Management OÜ
All rights reserved.

Author: Theodore Sinclair
ISBN HARDBACK: 978-1-80581-581-5
ISBN PAPERBACK: 978-1-80581-108-4
ISBN EBOOK: 978-1-80581-581-5

A Voyage Through Uncharted Bliss

On the beach with toes in sand,
A seagull droops, his lunch unplanned.
He dives for fries, not fish or chips,
While tourists spill their drinks in zips.

The sun dances high—what a sight!
A sunburned Santa, what a fright!
He juggles coconuts with glee,
As palm trees laugh, they shake like me.

A crab in shades tries to pose,
"I'm cooler than your hotdog nose!"
He saunters sideways, steals a look,
As folks unravel from their book.

At twilight's beck, the fireflies play,
A dog in shades claims it's his day.
He chases stars, a goofy blip,
Who knew bliss held such a quip?

Reflections on a Dreamy Lake

Silly ducks in feathered hats,
Waddle past with sassy chats.
A frog plays tunes on lily pads,
While fish swim by with winking fads.

The sun does dance, a disco ball,
While turtles take their leisurely crawl.
Bugs do break out in conga lines,
And crickets draft sweet party signs.

Colors of an Infinite Sunset

Sky paints pink a lopsided grin,
While clouds in polka dots join in.
A squirrel tries to juggle seeds,
But ends up in the tangled weeds.

The sun slips low, a lazy tease,
As fireflies play hide-and-seek with ease.
Rabbits hop in shades so bright,
While owls rehearse their stand-up night.

Where the Heart Finds Home

In cozy nooks where laughter grows,
A parrot wears a bow, you know!
Kittens plot in sunbeams' glow,
As puppies chase their tails below.

A hamster spins its wheel so fast,
While dreams of cheese make each day last.
The blender hums a kitchen tune,
As cookies dance by the light of the moon.

The Canvas of Endless Vistas

A painter's splash brings giggles near,
As flamingos sport shades, oh dear!
Mountains wear frosting hats of cream,
And rivers swirl in a candy dream.

Stars do nap on velvet skies,
While comets tease with dizzy flies.
The landscape sings with blushing flair,
As taffy trees sway without a care.

Seraphic Skies and Quiet Sands

Under skies so wide and blue,
Birds attempt to steal a shoe.
Seagulls squawk their playful yell,
While sandcastles start to swell.

Waves tumble in with laughter's sound,
A crab performs a dance profound.
Sunbathers roll, they twist and flop,
As ice cream melts with every plop.

Odes to the Swaying Palms

The palms are grooving, what a sight,
Shaking fronds in sheer delight.
A parrot drops a lime so bright,
And squirrels join, they take flight.

Cocktails spill and drench the ground,
While laughter flows, a joyous sound.
In hammocks swing, there's no big rush,
As sunburns creep, we scrunch and hush.

Enchantment in the Air

Magic's brewing in the breeze,
As flip-flops slide and wobbly knees.
A flamingo strolls with elegant flair,
While sunstarts burn without a care.

The sand's so hot, we jump and squeal,
In search of shade, it's quite the deal.
A picnic spread, a jumbled feast,
With ants in line, they come in beast.

The Spirit of Starlit Nights

Stars twinkle down, they chuckle bright,
As nightime critters join the flight.
A fire pit pops, marshmallows tease,
While friends tell jokes with utmost ease.

Moonlit paths invite a dance,
As we trip over, take a chance.
Ghost stories swirl, yet all delight,
In the glow of soft, celestial light.

Dreams Chasing the Setting Sun

In a hammock, I sway and dream,
Thoughts of tacos fill my scheme.
Sunlight drips like melting cheese,
While seagulls dance on ocean breeze.

Flip-flops squeak with every stroll,
Crabs scuttle like they're on a roll.
With each wave, laughter cascades,
In this paradise, the fun never fades.

The Quietude of Hidden Nooks

Secret corners, sunbeams delight,
Chasing lizards, what a sight!
A squirrel plotting snack attacks,
While I sip coconut from high stacks.

Mismatched socks on sandy feet,
In this haven, my life's a treat.
A ukulele plays silly tunes,
While soft clouds wear cotton costumes.

Honeyed Breeze of Divine Escape

The breeze whispers sweet nothings near,
Ice cream melts, and so does fear.
With every lick, a giggle bursts,
Life is peachy, or maybe worse!

Fluffy clouds wearing goofy grins,
Chasing dreams where laughter begins.
Fruits dance and join the sunny crew,
In this wild, fruity rendezvous!

Melodies Carried by the Wind

Jazzed-up crickets serenade night,
Stars twinkle with mischievous light.
A grasshopper plays the trumpet fine,
While I croak my best friend's favorite line.

With every breeze, the giggles rise,
Tickling toes and curious sighs.
The world spins in a goofy sway,
In this bright, absurd cabaret!

Infinite Skies Above

Up above, the clouds all smile,
Like fluffy sheep, they stretch a while.
Sunshine beams, a golden spree,
I lost my snack, it's in a tree!

Kites are dancing, flying high,
Playing tag with birds that fly.
Lost my wig to a gusty blow,
Hey look, it landed on a crow!

With friends in tow, we laugh and play,
Chasing shadows through the day.
A picnic spread, then ants arrive,
Sharing crumbs keeps us alive!

At twilight, jokes fill up the air,
We stumble, giggle, without a care.
Stars twinkle down, they're making fun,
Of our dance moves, everyone!

Mirage of Bliss

Waves are crashing, what a sound,
Floating drinks, where's mine I found?
Flip-flops flying, what a sight,
Guess I'm part of the sea tonight!

Sandy toes and salty chins,
Catching crabs, oh what a win!
But they scurry; I just stare,
Caught one in my beachy hair!

Seagulls squawk, they steal our fries,
With my sandwich, what a surprise!
Chasing them 'round like a silly dance,
Only to drop my pickle, what a chance!

Sunset dips in shades of gold,
We sing off-key, we're bold and bold.
Life's a joke, let's have a cheer,
As waves cheer back, taking us near!

Harmony in the Breeze

Butterflies flit, they tease my hat,
On a breeze, making me chat.
Picnic ants in perfect line,
"Please don't march on my snack divine!"

Lemonade spills, oh what a splash,
Giggles erupt, like a joyful clash.
Bubbles float, drift and wave,
They pop like dreams from the day we crave!

A game to catch the wind's soft hand,
We fall like leaves, on this fine land.
Sundrenched smiles spread with glee,
Is that a crab moving near me?

With every twist and laugh and try,
We spin beneath the wide blue sky.
Nothing serious, let's just play,
In our paradise, let's stay all day!

The Timeless Seaside

Time forgot us, with sandy feet,
As we build a castle, oh, what a feat!
Seashells scatter, all in a pile,
A treasure hunt with goofy style!

Fun in the sun, oh what a race,
To catch the tide, a slippery chase.
But waves are sneaky, they swirl and bite,
Drenched like fish, we laugh in delight!

Sunset whispers, colors a-bloom,
We twirl and whirl, like flowers in bloom.
But wait! A seagull makes its swoop,
To grab my sandwich, what a scoop!

With laughter echoing through the sand,
We dance like dervishes, hand in hand.
In this timeless hour, we will stay,
With hearts aglow, in merry play!

The Embrace of Infinite Horizons

The sun wears a funny hat,
As seagulls play peek-a-boo.
Sandy toes and giggles abound,
Life's a circus, who knew?

Turtles move like they're on break,
Beach balls bounce like rubber,
The waves are in a dance-off,
Even crabs can't help but flutter.

Strawberry ice cream on our cheeks,
Melting in the midday heat,
Laughter echoes with each splash,
While sunbathers wiggle their feet.

And just when we think we can't stand,
A wave crashes, and we are gone,
But each time we rise, a chuckle erupts,
Oh, how we love this daily dawn!

A Palette of Eternal Colors

The sky's got blues just that loud,
Like a parrot on a spree.
Paint it yellow, splash it red,
Nature's canvas, let it be!

The flowers gossip in orange tones,
Daisies twist with grace.
Even rocks form silly shapes,
As if they're in a race.

Umbrella drinks with little straws,
Sipped as we recline.
A crab wearing shades strolls by—
Guess he's a friend of mine!

Each sunset brings the giggles out,
Light dims, but joy won't quit.
Tomorrow brings a fresh palette,
For clowns of the ocean—wildly lit!

Shadowy Fables of Distant Lands

Beneath palm trees, stories bloom,
Squirrels plot their heist,
A coconut fell, what a boom!
It seemed rather unvised.

Mermaids giggle at our jokes,
While dolphins flip with flair.
Pirates search for golden groks,
But that's simply not fair!

The sand tells tales of baby frogs,
Hopping like they're on a mission.
With every leap, a chuckle logs,
Nature's own rendition.

As the shadows stretch and yawn,
The stars join in the fun,
With a wink they steal the show,
Another day has come undone!

Cadence of the Cosmic Dance

The stars are doing the cha-cha,
Moonlight spins with flair.
Planets play musical chairs,
While we chuckle in the air.

Asteroids roll like bowling balls,
Comets race like kids.
Black holes make the silliest faces,
In this grand cosmic biz.

Gravity pulls us into giggles,
As we float with ease.
Two aliens wave from afar,
And beg for one more tease!

In this dance of stellar dreams,
We prance without a care.
As laughter ripples through the cosmos,
Heaven's dance is ours to share!

Celestial Joy of Unwritten Stories

The sun hangs low, with no intent,
To set its course, so time is bent.
We sip on laughter, let worries fly,
As clouds float by like popcorn in the sky.

With each new dawn, a joke unfolds,
Like cheeky stars, our tales are bold.
Fruitful naps on lazy lawns,
Tickle fights till the break of dawn.

A butterfly winks, it flits around,
In this sweet chaos, joy is found.
Each moment drips with silly glee,
As if a jester's chair's our seat.

So let's embrace this joyful spree,
Amidst the blooms and buzzing bee.
For in this scene of wild delight,
A pinch of laughter keeps us light.

Minutes that Stretch Like Eternity

A clock that laughs at passing time,
Plays silly tricks, like a nursery rhyme.
Each tick a giggle, each tock a cheer,
As seconds dance without a fear.

We race the sun, but it stands still,
With winks and chuckles, it bends to our will.
A game of tag with shadows we play,
While silly squirrels plot their fray.

The ice cream melts, oh what a sight,
It drips and plops, pure delight!
We chase it down with wild delight,
As joyful cries fill the summer night.

The more we move, the slower time goes,
A riddle wrapped in a dreamlike pose.
In this vast stretch of gleeful scenes,
Our laughter weaves the softest dreams.

The Enchantment of Endless Evenings

The stars are gossiping, sly and bright,
As fireflies dance, igniting the night.
A picnic spread, with snacks galore,
As laughter echoes from the shore.

Moonlit shadows steal the show,
While marshmallows roast in a glow.
Our giggles float on the gentle breeze,
Sweet serenades from the rustling trees.

Time melts like butter on warm bread,
As stories swirl inside our heads.
Each sip of lemonade, a cheeky plot,
As we spin tales that twist and knot.

To the symphony of crickets we sway,
In this allure of twilight play.
With each passing hour, our smiles grow wide,
In this enchanted space, we take our ride.

Abode of Infinite Possibilities

The door swings wide, with endless glee,
A house where joy holds the master key.
Each room a riddle, painted bright,
Where nonsense reigns in pure delight.

In the kitchen, laughter simmers well,
With pies that tell a jolly tale.
The living room's a circus of fun,
As we juggle stories under the sun.

Under beds, where giggles hide,
In every nook, our dreams collide.
We dance through hallways, round and round,
In this abode where joy is found.

Each day's a page, unwritten, unscrolled,
A place where wild imaginations unfold.
So grab your hat, step inside this jest,
In the land of laughs, we're truly blessed.

Timeless Waves caressing Dreams

The sunniest sun smiles wide,
As seagulls tell their silly lies.
A crab wears shades, he's quite the dude,
While flip-flops dance in the warm breeze.

Shells gossip secrets from the shore,
While beach balls bounce like playful cats.
A mermaid sings, but oh, too loud,
And sunburned tourists do silly hats.

In coconut trees, iguanas chill,
Counting all the waves they've seen.
The ocean waves throw silly pranks,
While fish laugh it up, forming a scene.

As poets scribble rhymes in sand,
And little kids make castles grand.
Laughter fills the salty air,
Oh, the joy of life at hand!

When the Horizon Breathes

The horizon yawns, it's just too lazy,
Clouds are fluffier than a baby's hair.
A beach ball floats, oh how it's crazy,
While suntanned squirrels are brave to dare.

Chairs lounge around in the golden sun,
A cooldown splash! Oh, what a thrill!
With ice cream cones in a wobbly run,
Their drips are dancing down the hill.

Palm trees wobble like they're grooving,
As flip-flops sync up for a dance.
Tanned bodies, all mischief moving,
Chasing crabs with giddy prance.

When the horizon breathes out loud,
And sunsets spill laughter in a crowd.
Life's a comedy with ocean waves,
In this paradise we can't quite save!

Infinite Light Above the Ocean

Stars twinkle like they're playing cards,
While dolphins jump with such delight.
Beach towels spread out in funny yards,
Pineapple drinks make everything bright.

The moon hangs low, such a close friend,
As surfboards tease the ocean's might.
Silly shadows twist and bend,
In the dance of soft, dreamy night.

Crabs in tuxedos strut on the line,
Holding a soirée under the moon.
They toast to waves with a splash of brine,
And the stars hum a tune, oh so soon.

Fireflies giggle, lighting up glee,
As laughter sails across the bay.
With shimmering hope and a whimsical spree,
We cherish this night, come what may!

Tranquil Moments in Bliss

Laughing waves tickle our toes,
As sun-kissed cheeks glow with cheer.
Sandy footprints that nobody knows,
Lead to treasures we hold dear.

In shady spots, we tell jokes loud,
While picnic ants join the fun.
A kite's in the air, oh so proud,
Dancing with clouds, oh what a run!

Barefoot adventures, what a delight,
Chasing the breeze, like kids at play.
Tickling wrinkles, from laughter's height,
In this tranquil bliss, make it stay.

With every splash and sandcastle dream,
We gather chuckles, not just tan.
Paradise whispers and giggles gleam,
As joy paints colors, with no plan!

Eyes Closed to a World of Wonder

With eyes shut tight, I munch on pie,
A squirrel mocks me, oh my, oh my!
The sun bakes my thoughts to a soft pudding,
While giggling clouds dance, their joy so budding.

Here comes a bee, buzzing with cheer,
It steals my drink; how rude, I fear!
I chase it around, a wild notion,
In a world of chaos, I'm lost in motion.

The grass tickles toes in a playful way,
I nearly trip, but I laugh and stay,
The laughter of friends fills the warm air,
In this silly realm, we have not a care.

As the sunset stains sky a vibrant gold,
With stories of laughter, we dare be bold,
Each silly moment, a treasure we'd keep,
In a funny dream, we laugh and leap.

The Whisper of Softly Falling Leaves

Leaves tumble around, a colorful fight,
In their crisp chatter, I lose some height,
A gust of wind tosses me like a toy,
Oh, nature's giggles, such simple joy!

A leaf sticks to my nose like a badge,
I parade it proudly, feeling like a sage,
Squirrels roll by, plotting their prank,
While my dignity takes a tiny plank.

I twirl through the woods, dancing with glee,
A branch grabs my hat; how rude can it be?
The forest chuckles and sways in delight,
As I stumble and trip, losing my flight.

Under the trees, I find my true peace,
In this madcap world, our laughter won't cease,
With whispers of leaves guiding my way,
I embrace every blunder, come what may.

Nature's Embrace in Timeless Wonderland

Mushrooms are hats on a dance floor of grass,
Twirling and swirling, the critters all pass,
A rabbit wears shades, looks far too cool,
While I just sit back, feeling the fool.

The breeze whispers secrets, a tickle on skin,
A leaf lands on my head—oh where have I been?
I join in the laughter of butterflies bright,
In this wacky domain, every flower's a sight.

Clouds start a race; they're off in a blur,
I cheer them on with my wide-open slur,
The trees start to sway, their branches in cheer,
It's a funny parade, and I'm at the rear.

Here in this haven, the wild critters play,
Our shenanigans stretch through the sunlit day,
With smiles and giggles as bright as the sun,
In this whimsical world, we're all just having fun.

Lighthouses of Hope and Peace

On rocky cliffs, the lighthouse stands tall,
Screaming 'Enjoy life!' with its bright, beaming call,
I wave at the ocean, it splashes with glee,
The fish send their love, as they jump and flee.

Seagulls join in, quite the unwelcome crew,
Stealing my sandwich—what a hullabaloo!
I shout, 'Please return my lunch with grace!'
But they just squawk back, in their well-practiced place.

The tide comes in, a comedian's jest,
Turning my picnic to quite the wet fest,
I laugh and I dance, soaked to the bone,
In this goofy arena, I feel so at home.

As the twilight glows, laughter takes flight,
With stars peeking through, oh what a sight!
This haven's embrace holds peace at its core,
In this lighthouse world, we laugh evermore.

Nature's Hymn in Soft Glows

The sun wears shades of peach and gold,
While squirrels act like they are bold.
A butterfly flirts with a flower's nose,
As bees keep buzzing like they know a joke.

Laughter tickles the leaves on high,
As clouds float by, puffed like a pie.
The grass waves hello to the wandering feet,
While ants dance daily, a tiny beat.

The rivers giggle, they shimmer and sway,
Singing songs of mischief, come out and play!
A frog leaps in, with an oversized grin,
Making a splash, it's a splash-tastic win!

With nature's charm, every jest's sincere,
As monkeys swing, spreading silly cheer.
Beneath a sky so delightfully bright,
Joy and laughter make everything right.

Echoes of the Beyond

The clouds whisper secrets of silly dreams,
As stars joke around with their shiny beams.
A comet zips by, with a wink and a nudge,
For earthlings below, they can only judge.

In moonlit patches, shadows prance,
Bounding about like they're in a dance.
Whispers of wind tell tales so grand,
Of llamas in tuxedos on a foreign land.

Galaxies giggle, each twinkle a laugh,
Making stardust strut, what a glowing path!
The universe chuckles, quite full of glee,
As planets play hide and seek, oh so carefree!

Echoes of laughter float through the night,
Spreading joy with that shimmering light.
So come all ye dreamers, let's share in this show,
With humor and glee, let imaginations grow!

Tides of Emotion in Stillness

The waves roll in with a playful clap,
Telling tales of a sea star's map.
Dolphins spin tales, somersault high,
While fish wear hats, oh my, oh my!

Seagulls squawk with a comical flair,
As they argue over who gets the fairest share.
A crab scuttles by in its own little way,
Wearing a crown made of driftwood all day.

The sand tickles toes, a delightful tease,
As beach balls soar with a cool summer breeze.
With laughter that echoes along the shore,
The ocean sings songs forevermore.

So let's gather shells and build silly towers,
While sunlight dances and brightens our hours.
In this realm of fun and oceanic play,
We'll cherish the joy of each whimsical day!

The Magical Embrace of Silken Skies

Up in the air, the balloons take flight,
Waving goodbye to clouds with delight.
A kite plays tag with the giggling breeze,
Tickling the sun through the rustling trees.

The rainbow grins with a colorful glow,
As rain plays hide and seek down below.
A blimp jokes 'round like it's lost in thought,
While fireflies wink, like ideas caught.

The moon throws a party, all stars are invited,
With jokes and laughter, everyone's delighted.
A comet breathes fire with a wink in its tail,
As night wraps itself in a whimsical veil.

So dance in the skies where dreams never stall,
And find joy and laughter in the magic of all.
For life's a grand circus, an ongoing show,
Where smiles and giggles forever will flow.

Tides of the Heart

Waves crash in my coffee cup,
While seagulls try to wake me up.
Surfboards tangled in the breeze,
My hair looks like a spaghetti tease.

Beach balls bounce down sandy trails,
Underneath, my flip-flops fail.
A crab in a tuxedo struts so proud,
I wish I could join his crabbie crowd.

The sun insists on stealing hats,
While I dodge tan lines like pesky gnats.
Picnic ants bring us a feast,
Who knew bugs could be such a beast?

As dusk descends, we swap our tales,
Of splashing waves and wobbly sails.
And just like that, we lose track of time,
In this goofy, upside-down paradigm.

Radiant Dreams

When stars come out, I ride a kite,
In dreams I dance, a silly sight.
The moon plays tricks on my silly brain,
Whispering jokes while I entertain.

Clouds wear hats, and trees wave hello,
While I trip over my own shadow.
Dreaming I'm a sandwich with jam,
Sliced by a toaster, how could I scram?

Fishes teach me the art of swim,
While jellybeans float just on a whim.
I giggle at planets wearing shoes,
In this dreamland, I can't lose!

The sun sneezes bright and clears the night,
And I chase stars, oh what a fright!
When morning comes, I'll shake my head,
With a grin, I greet my joyful bed.

Dappled Sunshine

Sunbeams play tag on my porch swing,
While squirrels argue about bling-bling.
The daisies wink, wearing their crowns,
While I'm tripping over my own clowns.

Butterflies laugh at my ukulele tune,
As ants host a party under the moon.
I squirt lemonade like a garden hose,
And get splashed by the neighbor's garden hose.

Lines at the ice cream stand stretch so wide,
I order a scoop, but they slip and slide.
Scoops tumble down like comical heaps,
While I giggle, ignoring their peeps.

Fruits chase each other upon my cake,
With sprinkles that dance like they're awake.
A slice of joy is what I crave,
In each dappled ray, I feel so brave.

The Abode of Wonder

In fields of socks, I nibble on cheese,
While balloons float off, dancing with ease.
A rabbit wears glasses, counting my hops,
As socks and sandwiches do their flips and flops.

Marshmallow clouds drift over my head,
With giggles and tickles stitched in their thread.
Every door leads to places unknown,
Where pinatas burst out like seeds that have grown.

The wind tells jokes, tickling my face,
As I tumble about in this whimsical place.
I chase after giggles and bubbles galore,
Finding treasures that never were before.

With each twist and turn of the hour,
Joy plants its roots, like a delicate flower.
In this abode where the silly skies blend,
Life's a laugh that never seems to end.

A Tapestry of Stars Unfolds

In a hammock strung so high,
With snacks that somehow fly,
Jellybeans dance on my nose,
While a parrot strikes a pose.

Sipping juice that's way too sweet,
Caught a crab with fancy feet,
He winked and gave a little cheer,
I'm pretty sure he wants a beer.

A sunburned dolphin gives a wink,
As I accidentally sink,
Into the waves, oh what a trip,
Goodbye, goodbye, my tasty chip!

Stars twinkle, night is here,
A squirrel drops a watermelon sphere,
With laughter echoing through the night,
In this surreal, absurd delight.

Shores of Everlasting Comfort

On the shore, where sand meets toe,
I found a crab doing the limbo,
He taught me moves I can't complete,
Now I dance with two left feet.

Beach balls bouncing in the air,
While seagulls plot—it's hardly fair,
They dive for chips with cunning flair,
And leave me with a soggy chair.

Sunsets splash like paint on the sea,
But I just spilled my drink on me,
With laughter ringing through the dusk,
I guess it's time to rename this musk!

Stars arrive, with a wink and grin,
As crabs and I strike up a din,
Dancing shadows with shells in tow,
In a paradise where silliness can grow.

The Lullaby of Distant Seas

A whale sings in a jazzy tune,
While octopuses jive to the moon,
Mermaids giggle in frothy waves,
Crafting shells for their silly graves.

The sun brings out the clumsy crew,
With flip-flops stuck like a glue,
One slips and lands on a dolphin's back,
Hey buddy, the ocean's not a track!

Seashells speak in riddles today,
As crabs engage in a muscle display,
With muscle-flexing and silly snaps,
I can't stop chuckling, oh, perhaps!

Nightfall drapes a silly hat,
Where jellyfish dance like acrobats,
Every moment, pure delight,
As laughter echoes into the night.

Days Bathed in Golden Glow

In golden light, the sunbeam plays,
Playing hide and seek for days,
A lizard dons a tiny hat,
As I chat with a curious cat.

Kites fly high, in loops and spins,
While I fumble with my whirly pins,
A gust of wind takes my last chip,
Now it's swimming for my snack trip!

Bubbles float like dreams untold,
As rubber ducks show off their bold,
They waddle while I take the plunge,
In this paradise, all rules we grunge!

At day's end, the sun waves goodbye,
My beach towel's lost in a pie-sky,
With giggles and grins, the fun won't cease,
In this wild, absurd, blissful peace!

Lullabies of the Dreamscape

In the land where giggles bloom,
Bouncing gnomes with green hats loom.
Silly clouds that dance and prance,
Tickle the stars; they join the dance.

Bumblebees wear striped pajamas,
While sheep jump over wide-brimmed llamas.
Butterflies sip tea with a smile,
Sipping nonsense, staying a while.

Ducks wearing sunglasses waddle along,
Singing a comical, chirpy song.
Cacti wear socks, so bright and bold,
In a world where laughter never gets old.

Dreamers drift on candy-floss clouds,
Each one laughing, hilariously loud.
In this realm, oddities reign,
Where silly shadows dance in the rain.

Time's Gentle Embrace

Tick-tock of hours sound so sweet,
Dancing turtles on tiny, warm feet.
With every yawn, the sun takes a nap,
While moonlight folds in a cozy wrap.

Socks lost in the laundry rally 'round,
Hosting parades, no one's ever found.
Each minute spins like a gleeful kite,
In a loop of giggles, feeling just right.

Pancake flippers juggle the task,
Throwing butter like it's too much to ask.
Each bite's a treasure, syrupy glaze,
In this sweet, silly, charmed place.

Time wears pajamas, laughs in the breeze,
Sipping its coffee with whimsical ease.
Every moment is a playful phrase,
In a world that's lost in whimsical ways.

Celestial Shores

Stars play hopscotch on sandy waves,
With fish that wear sparkly little knaves.
Jellyfish drift in a jelly-like glee,
Sipping starlight, feeling fancy-free.

Seashells whisper sailor's old jokes,
While octopuses dance, hilarious folks.
Turtles wear boas, parading with flair,
Under the moon, they twist in the air.

Gulls don top hats and spin on their toes,
While dolphins play tag with a splishy-splash pose.
The ocean giggles with bubbly surprise,
As crabs in tuxedos compete for the prize.

Here in this cove of playful delight,
Where silliness reigns through day and night.
Every splash brings laughter in scores,
On these whimsical celestial shores.

Sunlit Memories

Sunbeams tickle the daisies so bright,
While ants play chess, each move a delight.
Grasshoppers leap with comical flair,
While butterflies spin in the sun-kissed air.

Daydreams bounce on trampoline skies,
With popsicles melting and children's sly sighs.
Each hour is painted with bright colors true,
As giggles float high, like a balloon zoo.

Kites chase the wind with a fluttery dance,
While butterflies wink, and insects prance.
Memories sparkle like confetti in play,
In this sunny world, we frolic away.

On trails of laughter, we run hand in hand,
With a piñata of dreams in this whimsical land.
Every moment is a treasure that beams,
As we wander through life, lost in our dreams.

A Symphony of Radiant Mornings

In the dawn's embrace, I chase my shoe,
A squirrel steals my coffee, what can I do?
Sunbeams tickle my sleepy face,
While birds announce a very loud race.

The toast is dancing, my jam takes flight,
Butterflies mock me, such a silly sight.
A parade of ants march to the beat,
As I juggle pancakes—oh, what a feat!

A friendly breeze winks, "Don't you dare frown!"
With laughter a'leaping, I chase it around.
The world feels goofy, bright and untamed,
A carnival morning, where fun is proclaimed.

So here's to the laughs in the sun's gentle glow,
With hiccups and giggles, we all steal the show!
Forget all the worries, just dance like a fool,
In this merry morning, where joy is the rule.

Celestial Glow of Dusk's Arrival

As twilight descends, my snacks all collide,
A sandwich serenade—oh, what a ride!
Fireflies boogie, they shine just like stars,
While crickets breakdance and munch on my bars.

The shadows play tricks, a grand puppet show,
"Who's that sneaking up?"—my dog's in the flow.
With goofy grins, we jump and we pop,
Underneath the glow, we're ready to stop!

The moon starts its giggle, the world gives a cheer,
A tickle of laughter, as nighttime draws near.
Stars stick their tongues out, a cosmic ballet,
In this whimsical dusk, we forever will play.

"Oh look at that one! A pumpkin so bright!"
A comet, I think—what a curious sight!
We dance in the gloam, letting worries all sway,
In this spirited twilight that keeps gloom at bay.

Embracing the Warmth of Twilight

In the twilight's arms, there's a glow so sweet,
My feet are lost somewhere under this heat.
Marshmallows giggle, they roast by the fire,
While we harmonize with songs of desire.

The shadows are silly, they stretch and they bend,
My friends spill their drinks—but we just pretend!
Laughter erupts as the stars twitch with glee,
The moon winks at us, oh, what joy it will be!

With blankets like capes, we're heroes tonight,
S'mores in our pockets, oh what a sight!
The wind whispers secrets, tickles my chin,
In this cozy hour, let the night begin!

So let's twirl and whirl till the morning arrives,
With giggles and charms, where our humor thrives.
Under the canopy of dreams flying high,
In this twilight magic, we'll soar through the sky.

Gentle Echoes of Paradise Lost

In a garden of giggles, where flowers might tease,
A bee steals my hat while I'm trying to sneeze.
The butterflies chuckle as I try to chase,
Funny how nature moves at a quick pace.

The trees tell me stories, a comical shoo,
While squirrels rehearse for their next big debut.
I trip on a root, now that's quite a plot,
"Hey, ground, you funny—give me a shot!"

The sun waves goodbye, but the laughter remains,
As rain patters lightly, it sings through the lanes.
With puddles like mirrors, we splash on the go,
In this whimsical world, let the good vibes flow!

So here's to the quirks and the fumbles we share,
With joyful mischief, we float in the air.
In this space of delight, where memories gleam,
We'll dance through the echoes and ride on a dream.

The Allure of Moonlit Waters

Under the glow, fish dance around,
While seagulls squawk like they own the sound.
Flip-flops are flung, popcorn spills with glee,
Laughter erupts, oh, just let it be!

The moon grins wide, a playful sphere,
Lovers trip over, yet they persevere.
Splashing in waves, their secrets unfold,
With each silly blunder, more stories are told!

A crab on a mission, pinching my toe,
'Hey buddy, that's rude!' I yell with a glow.
The night stretches on, filled with delight,
As wiggles and jiggles pace through the night.

Beneath starry skies, together we feast,
On snacks that we know are far from the least.
A dance-off ensues, with a coconut twist,
In moonlit waters, who could resist?

A Horizon Awash in Dreams

A bright sun awakens, I stretch and I yawn,
Too bright for my eyes, it's a brand-new dawn.
The horizon winks with a cheeky little grin,
Saying, 'Come now, let the fun begin!'

Jumping in sand, oh what a mad race,
Flip in the air, land right on my face!
Giggles erupt from all around,
As I bury my friend in a sandy mound.

A seagull swoops down, looking for fries,
I wave my arms, their laughter still flies.
With kites in the breeze and laughter so bright,
Only silly moments fill our daylight.

As the sun starts to fade, we crack open drinks,
Spilling them here, oh, what do you think?
With hearts full of joy, this paradise stays,
Tomorrow is surely another fun maze!

The Lure of Close-Knit Shores

At a beach where the waves tend to chuckle and play,
I found a lost sandal—what a strange day!
Tossed to a seagull, my perfect plan,
He merely squawked, took off, not a fan.

Sand castles rise, oh, what a fine sight,
Each tower deflating with every wave's bite.
We stand with our shovels, like kings with a throne,
As the tide steals our castle and leaves us alone.

A frisbee goes flying, oh what a brief flight,
It whacks an old lady—oh what a delight!
She laughs like a sister, not bothered a bit,
This close-knit shore, it just feels like a hit!

Beneath swaying palms, we feast on our score,
Hot dogs and laughter, who needs anything more?
As the sun dips low, our smiles are wide,
A day with my friends is a joy I can't hide.

The Passage of Serene Hours

Time crawls like a turtle, without a care to race,
As I sip my drink, my toes in the lace.
A hammock swings low, with each lazy sway,
I nod off to dreamland, for just one short stay.

A lobster named Larry claims my favorite chair,
I shoo him away, but he just doesn't care.
With shells on the ground, our giggles arise,
As we dodge and weave, what a comical surprise!

The clock's on a mission to mess with our fun,
As I dare it to move, it just sits like the sun.
Time's supposed to fly, yet here it just stalls,
In this silly realm, laughter echoes and calls.

As twilight descends, we gather our cheer,
With stories to tell, we toast to the year.
In every shared moment, so precious and rare,
The passage of hours, we blissfully share!

Rhythms of a Tranquil Day

Beneath the sun, we dance with glee,
Our ice cream cones melt, oh how they flee.
The hammock sways, a friendly beast,
As we try to nap, but laughter won't cease.

The birds sing tunes that tease our ears,
While we play cards and sip cold beers.
A squirrel steals lunch and makes a mess,
Chasing it off, we feel quite blessed.

The clock ticks slow, but what is time?
We invent new games, and they're sublime.
A race in flip-flops, who can wobble best?
We fall flat, giggling is our quest.

So here we are, in this sunny play,
Every moment's silly, come what may.
With friends beside us, oh what a treat,
In this paradise, life is oh-so-sweet!

Sun-kissed Moments in Time

Golden rays beam down with laughter,
We chase the shadows, what comes after?
Your hat flies off, a comical sight,
You trip on sand, but hold on tight!

A picnic spread, but ants have come,
They carry our snacks, oh isn't that fun?
We build a fortress made of towels,
Pretend to rule, while the seagulls howl.

A splash in waves becomes a dance,
You take a tumble, what a chance!
With water guns, we wage a war,
In this silly battle, who keeps score?

As sunsets paint the sky in hues,
We find our way to evening's muse.
Stories unfold, with giggles and sighs,
In these sun-kissed moments, laughter never dies.

Beneath the Canopy of Bliss

Underneath branches, we lay and dream,
The world fades away, or so it would seem.
A breeze whispers secrets we can't quite hear,
While snacks scatter, oh dear, oh dear!

We spot a squirrel, it's quite the spy,
Stealing our cookies as we both sigh.
You throw a chip, it jumps in fright,
Now it's an acrobat under the light.

Clouds drift by, we name them all,
Is that a dragon? Or maybe a ball?
Our laughter echoes like a playful song,
Time dances lightly, but feels so long.

With each silly tale, the hours fly,
In our leafy haven, we can't deny.
This joy-filled bubble, oh what a bliss,
A world of whimsy, we wouldn't miss.

Gentle Ripples of Memory

By the pond's edge, we toss a stone,
Splashing laughter in tones of our own.
The ducks quack back, they're in on the joke,
As we share tales, with every poke.

Your hat's afloat—oh what a sight!
We rush to rescue with all our might.
But slipping on mud, who can resist?
We're covered in goo; that's how we exist!

We cast our lines, hoping for fish,
Instead, we catch moments—now that's the wish!
A tug at the line, what do we find?
Just seaweed tangled, but we're intertwined.

As day starts to fade, we sigh with delight,
With goofy grins, we'll remember this night.
In the ripples of time, we laughed 'til we cried,
In the heart of our paradise, where joy is our guide.

A Palette of Tranquility

In the sun, we cook and bake,
A pie, oh no! I made a flake.
The birds all laugh, they chirp and tease,
While I dive for crumbs, as quick as you please.

The hammock's swaying, I take a swing,
A snack, a nap, it's my sort of fling.
But look out! Here comes a sneaky bee,
I'll dance like mad, just to stay free!

The flowers giggle with petal grin,
A dance-off starts, let the fun begin!
I twirl and laugh, I trip on grass,
But what a joy! I'll never pass.

With each new breeze, the sunbeams play,
I chase my hat that's gone astray.
No worries here, just silliness bright,
In this bloom, I'm truly light!

Chasing the Light

With sunglasses on, I strut the sand,
My sunscreen bottle, oh so grand.
I leap to splash, in waves so cool,
But watch out, friend! Here comes the pool!

My piña colada's gone awry,
A coconut cup flies, oh my, oh my!
As seagulls squawk, they steal my fries,
I chase them down with silly cries.

The sun dips low, the colors swirl,
I trip on flip-flops, give a twirl.
With laughter bubbling, we gather round,
In this goofy stance, joy's always found.

The light fades slow, but we're not done,
We play charades and giggle for fun.
With each silly move, my heart takes flight,
In a fit of joy, we dance through the night!

Unfading Echoes of Joy

A morning stretch, the coffee brews,
I spill my cup, oh what a ruse!
The cat jumps high, what a surprise,
His pounce lands me with sleepy eyes.

On this bright lane, the kite takes flight,
But so do my fries, from my lunch bite.
Chasing them down with giggles and glee,
Come back, sweet snack, you belong with me!

The world spins fast on this merry gas,
Each clumsy step feels like a pass.
With a playful hop and a happy dive,
I'll sway to the rhythm, truly alive.

The sun dips low, we gather near,
In fits of laughter, we hold each cheer.
In this sweet ruckus, we find our song,
In a melody of joy where we belong.

Starlit Serenity

Under the moon, we toast with cheer,
A marshmallow mishap, oh dear, oh dear!
The fire pops, we duck and squeal,
S'mores on our heads, now that's a meal!

As stars twinkle bright, we circle tight,
I tell a joke, it's a silly sight.
My punchline flops, but laughter soars,
We bounce with glee, like swings and roars.

We prank the shadows, give them names,
While dancing 'round with silly games.
In the glow of night, we spin and sway,
A wacky crew, come what may.

The night may fade, but joy's alive,
With memories made, our spirits thrive.
In the starlit glow, we find our place,
A comedy of dreams, in time and space.

A Dance with the Waves

The waves invite a silly jig,
With splashes that make seagulls gig.
In flip-flops flying, we twirl and spin,
Laughing as sand sticks to our skin.

A crab joins in, a funky dancer,
Pinching toes, oh what a prancer!
We skip and hop like kids at play,
While the sun shines bright, oh hip-hip-hooray!

Moments Beyond Measure

Time wobbles like a jellyfish,
Each hour a spark of sheer bliss.
Tick-tock's a prankster, laughs with glee,
While we dance along, oh can't you see?

Ice cream spills, a splatter of joy,
Face full of chocolate, could there be a ploy?
Moments like these can't be counted or weighed,
Just grab a spoon—let's go on parade!

The Garden of Elysium

In a garden where daisies talk,
They giggle and gossip as we walk.
A sunflower grins, shades his face,
While bees make a buzz, a zany race!

We prune the jokes and weed the puns,
Watering laughter under the suns.
Each petal holds a punchline wait,
Let's harvest smiles—oh, isn't it great?

Kaleidoscope of Bliss

Colors swirl like a swirling dream,
A world where giggles reign supreme.
A parrot shouts, 'Polly wants a snack!'
As we paint the sky, no looking back!

Joy's a canvas, splattered and wild,
Every shade recalls the heart of a child.
With bubblegum clouds and laughter's cheer,
We'll dance through the colors, year after year!

Meadows Wrapped in Soft Embrace

In fields so wide, we roll and play,
Chasing butterflies that lead us astray.
Dreams are as fluffy as clouds on high,
We giggle as daisies wave us goodbye.

Sunshine tickles as we lay on grass,
Laughter echoes, oh, how the hours pass!
We dodge the bees, with a skip and a hop,
In this soft embrace, we never want to stop.

With sandwiches juggled and lemonade spills,
We count the ants and their wild little thrills.
Should we take a nap? Nah, just one more run!
Time plays tricks, as if it's just for fun.

Each twirl and twist is a dose of delight,
While we race the sunset, oh what a sight!
The meadows remain our giggling stage,
In this blissful realm, we turn every page.

The Mirage of Forever

We search for dreams in the shimmering glow,
But find only picnics where the ants like to show.
Our quest for a fountain that grants every wish,
Ends with a pizza and a deep, cheesy dish.

The sun throws its rays like confetti in air,
While we sit wondering if we'd ever dare
To chase after rainbows, or slide down a hill,
Instead we settle for snacks and a thrill.

The hours stretch long like a lazy old cat,
With each purr and stretch, we tip our hat.
A mirage of laughter dances in the heat,
But who would trade for a banana split sweet?

"Forever" we giggle, until we hit snooze,
Unraveling plans as we fight off the blues.
The mirage is real if you look through the glass,
And in this funny tale, we make moments last.

Serenade of the Gentle Breeze

The breeze sings softly, with a tickle and tease,
Carrying secrets of low-flying bees.
We hum along, as the grass starts to sway,
Joking that it's nature's musical play.

With ice cream cones slipping, oh what a sight!
We laugh as they drop, in the warm sunlight.
Moments like these, filled with giggles and grins,
Are treasures we keep, where the fun never thins.

Kites dance above like they're learning to fly,
While we lay beneath, reaching out to the sky.
The serenade whispers, "This is the life,"
As we plot our next prank with a dollop of strife.

With every soft breeze, our laughter takes flight,
We write silly songs under twinkling twilight.
So here's to the moments, like bubbles that rise,
In this sweet serenade, we wear our surprise.

The Dance of Shadows and Sunlight

Shadows long and playful, they twist and they twirl,
In a theater of giggles, our joy starts to whirl.
We dance with the light, like a game of tag,
Bumping into bushes, never feeling a drag.

When the sun takes a bow, and the dusk starts to hum,
We waltz with the twilight, hoping time won't come.
Footprints in sand are the stories we leave,
While the breeze taunts us, "Who would dare to grieve?"

Chasing our shadows, we try to keep pace,
In this quirky contest, who'll win the race?
Smiles are contagious, and laughter ignites,
As we mix the two, shadows dance with delights.

So we sway and we spin, on this silver-lit floor,
Where each fleeting moment is never a chore.
The dance unfolds, as the moon takes its place,
A funny affair, we all embrace in grace.

Joy in Every Grain of Sand

Upon the beach, we trip and slip,
Our toes all covered, oh what a grip!
Seagulls laugh as they swoop and dive,
While we search for shells, feeling alive.

Buckets and shovels, the kids do race,
Building castles, a sandy embrace.
Watch the tide come in, what a surprise,
Our fort now a moat, oh how time flies!

Ice cream drips down our sun-soaked arms,
Sticky fingers, oh such lovely charms!
Sandy dogs roll in their watery bliss,
Chasing their tails, they'd never miss.

The sun sets low with a wink and grin,
As we pack up, the fun won't thin.
Back to the car, we sing and sway,
Oh, how we love this silly play!

The Unbroken Spell

In the sun, we dance to silly tunes,
With seafood feasts beneath the moons.
Uncle Joe slips, falls in a tray,
While everyone laughs, 'Oh what a day!'

The parrot squawks, a weird old sage,
Reciting lines from a dog-eared page.
We roll our eyes but can't help but cheer,
A talking bird can't help but endear.

Lemonade spills as we splash and play,
Tanning mishaps make for a long stay.
The sunscreen wars, oh what a fight,
With greasy hands, we wave goodnight.

Under starlit skies, we tell tall tales,
Of mermaids, pirates, and wind-blown sails.
With laughter that echoes and gives a thrill,
We'll cherish these moments, come wind or chill!

Eternal Sunlit Shores

Sandy feet tangled in sunbeam dreams,
Where laughter bounces like playful beams.
Chasing the tide, we wave and shout,
In this blissful race, we can't fall out.

Umbrellas flop like tired old clowns,
As we sip coconut drinks in towns.
A crab scuttles by with a wiggle and tease,
While a gull tries to steal our hot dog please!

Caught in a game of toss and splash,
Even our sandals are prone to a crash.
The sand between toes, a gritty delight,
Each giggle and grin, a true sheer sight.

The sun dips down with a teasing glare,
To say goodnight while we don't care.
For unfading joy is our spirited goal,
As the waves remind us to dance with soul!

Whispering Palms of Serenity

Beneath the palms, we recline and sway,
With fruity drinks, we lounge all day.
A squirrel steals a chip right from my hand,
Oh, mischievous party in this land!

Tanning oil spills, what a sticky fate,
We find ourselves in a coconut crate.
"Help!" says my friend as she laughs out loud,
Stuck in the shade, she's quite the crowd!

A hammock swings like a gentle lullaby,
As we plan adventures that by and by.
A sea of bright colors, our vibrant parade,
Each memory made, like magic, will fade.

As night draws close, the stars start to gleam,
We trade our tales for a soft moonbeam.
In this charming chaos where laughter flows,
We breathe in joy, as the sweet sea breezes blow!

Eternal Sunsets

The sun spills juice on the ocean wide,
Colors splat like paint on a joyful ride.
Beach chairs are chairs that never say no,
Laughter bounces high, oh what a show!

Seagulls play poker, they're quite the team,
Winning with sandcastles, living the dream.
We toast to the tide, with drinks on a tray,
Wishing forever was just one more day!

Flip-flops are dancing, they sway and prance,
As crabs do the cha-cha, oh what a chance!
Flip over a coconut, find some surprise,
A tiny umbrella, it's all in the vibes!

The stars come out, but still there's the glow,
From a blender that sings, it steals the show.
The night is a party, the fun never halts,
We giggle and grin, while the moon does waltz!

Whispers of the Ocean

Waves are gossiping, secrets in the breeze,
Shells are eavesdropping, with mischievous tease.
The tide tickles toes, with a playful splish,
While seaweed sings songs—oh, what a dish!

Crabs wear tuxedos, heading to the ball,
Dancing on the shore, they're having a ball.
Fish hold a banquet, with snacks in a tray,
"Who ordered the plankton?" they laugh and sway!

Sandy toes beg for ice cream galore,
Top it with sprinkles—who could want more?
Turtles mediate a debate on food,
"Where's the best pizza? We're all in the mood!"

Seagull on the mic, with a stand-up routine,
Telling all the jokes, really quite the scene.
With laughter as high as the whispering sea,
Every little moment just tickles with glee!

The Endless Horizon

The horizon is winking, a cheeky old thing,
With clouds like fluffy cupcakes ready to fling.
Sailing on a wink, with a blink and a giggle,
The sun wears a hat, and it's starting to wiggle!

A dolphin pops up, with a splash and a twist,
Claiming it can dance, oh don't let it be missed!
Seashells are clapping in rhythm so tight,
As the gulls form a choir to sing through the night!

Surfboards are lounging, soaking up rays,
Painting the sea in a million fun ways.
As waves come in funny, a splash and a tune,
Joy swims through the deep under the smiling moon!

As stretchers and floats fight for sun-lounge space,
Water fights break out in this carefree place.
Friends shout, "We're sunburned!" with laughter ablaze,
This paradise giggles in whimsical ways!

Sunkissed Reverie

Sunshine gives high-fives to every little thing,
While flip-flops are singing and starting to swing.
Sandcastles wear crowns made of laughter and cheer,
Guarded by crabs puffing up their little sphere!

Bikini tops twirl, as dance-offs take flight,
With jellyfish DJs spinning tunes through the night.
Lemons and limes join in for the toast,
Toasting to palm trees, they are everyone's host!

A hammock sways lightly, a cozy cocoon,
Where sunbeams are drifting like kids on a balloon.
Ice cream melts faster than stories unfold,
Each scoop is a giggle, oh how the day's gold!

The stars blink alive, in playful surprise,
Wishes float up, like kites in the skies.
In this breezy laughter, life spins its thread,
With every soft heart, happy dreams are fed!

Saltwater Secrets and Sandy Footprints

The beach towel whispers loud and clear,
As seagulls squawk and steal my beer.
My flip-flops dance in the salty breeze,
While crabs plot schemes, oh what a tease!

Buckets and shovels, castles so grand,
Yet both wash away, just like my plan.
I dig for treasures, find only shells,
And tales of sunburn and sunscreen smells.

In the water, I flail like a fish on land,
While dolphins snicker at my awkward strand.
Sand in my shorts and a smile so wide,
These are the moments I take in stride.

So here I bask in absurd delight,
With beach ball bounces that take flight.
Every wave's a laugh, each tide a game,
In this seaside circus, I stake my claim.

The Horizon Where Hearts Converge

Barefoot romance with an ice cream cone,
Melting quickly, oh what a moan!
We giggle and laugh, hearts a-flutter,
While birds steal fries, how rude of them, mutter!

Sunset dates that never recede,
With laughter as bright as the flowers we'd seed.
But who stole my towel, oh what a crime!
It's just a beach day, don't waste my prime!

Conversations as salty as the waves,
With tales of suns and snorkeling caves.
In this slice of bliss, it's hard not to grin,
Even the waves stop to hear our din.

So here we dance on this sandy stage,
With flip-flops flying, we're quite the page!
Heartbeats echo as the stars align,
Caught in a moment that feels like divine.

Radiance of a Thousand Sunrises

At dawn, I fumble for my sunscreen tube,
While the seagulls laugh, 'Get in the groove!'
The sun peeks up, just a cheeky glare,
And I trip on my towel, oh do I dare!

With coffee spills and giggles that wake,
I chase after waves, oh what a mistake!
Splashing and slipping, I feel like a clown,
As my beach hat takes flight and heads for town.

But watch the sky brush with colors bright,
Pink and orange, oh what a sight!
As dolphins leap and do their dance,
I can't help but join in this wave romance.

So let the radiance steal the day,
With laughter echoing in a playful way.
Each sunrise a gift, a jubilant cheer,
In this paradise, I'll shed every fear.

A Journey Through Lingering Moments

With my towel packed and a snack in hand,
I venture forth to this sun-kissed land.
Each grain of sand tells tales of fun,
While sunscreen battles the morning sun.

Splashes and giggles paint the sea,
As waves crash and tickle my knee.
Footprints wash away, but laughter remains,
In this giddy moment, where joy reigns.

The sun dips low, and shadows grow tall,
Yet still, my laughter, it echoes through all.
A dance with seaweed, a laugh with a crab,
In each silly moment, I'm glad I'm fab.

As stars twinkle bright and the moon takes charge,
I cherish the antics, the joys, the large.
In this quirky journey, oh how we roam,
Finding paradise feels just like home.

www.ingramcontent.com/pod-product-compliance
Lightning Source LLC
Chambersburg PA
CBHW072124070526
44585CB00016B/1549